An Insider's View of Jesus

An Insider's View of Jesus

Video-Driven Discussions on Real Discipleship

Featuring Ted & Lee Comedy
Leader's Guide By Todd Temple

ZONDERVAN™

GRAND RAPIDS, MICHIGAN 49530 USA

An Insider's View of Jesus Leader's Guide: Video Driven Discussions on Real Discipleship

Copyright © 2003 Youth Specialties

Youth Specialties Books, 300 South Pierce Street, El Cajon, California 92020, are published by Zondervan Publishing House, 5300 Patterson Avenue Southeast, Grand Rapids, Michigan 49530.

Library of Congress Cataloging-in-Publication Data

Temple, Todd, 1958-
  An insider's view of Jesus leader's guide : video driven discussions
on real discipleship / by Todd Temple.
        p. cm.
  ISBN 0-310-24623-7 (pbk.)
  1.   Jesus Christ--Person and offices--Study and teaching. 2.   Christian
education of teenagers.   I. Title.
  BT207 .T46 2003
  268'.433--dc21

                                        2002012244

Web site addresses listed in this book were current at the time of publication. Please contact Youth Specialties via e-mail (YS@YouthSpecialties.com) to report URLs that are no longer operational and replacement URLs if available.

Edited by Linda Bannan and Rick Marschall

Cover design by Art Parts

Interior design by razdezignz

Production Assistance by Nicole Davis

Printed in the United States of America

02 03 04 05 06 07 /✤CH/ 10 9 8 7 6 5 4 3 2 1

For live performance and product information on TED & LEE:
Call toll-free 866-ARMADILLO (866-276-2345) or log on to www.TedandLee.com.

Table of Contents

Start Here

Intro

When I read the gospels I catch myself wondering why the disciples are so ... well, clueless. Time and again, they fail to catch what their Teacher is saying. And when they do catch it, there's a good chance they'll drop it in the next scene. Why is it that the teachings that are so clear to me leave the disciples scratching their heads? Am I smarter than the Teacher's favorite students?

No. Just better prepared. I've heard hundreds of sermons on Jesus' teachings. Taken seminary courses. Read the writings of some of the sharpest theologians in Christendom. I've had plenty of time to study and review, visit and revisit these lessons. And two thousand years' worth of tutors to help me.

The disciples had none of this. There were no Christian preachers but Jesus himself. No Sunday schools or seminaries. And no Christian books until they themselves wrote them years later. All they had was Jesus himself. So they followed and watched and listened, and tried to comprehend it all. In real time.

Given their Teacher's curious educational style, this was no easy feat. Let's face it: Some of his lessons *are* a bit difficult to follow. No lesson titles, key points, cute acrostics, objectives, outlines or handouts. Instead of using a blackboard, he writes in the dirt. And just when you think he's talking about one thing, he throws in a parable that seems to speak of something else. For his active learning, he tells the disciples to do things that are ridiculous or impossible, then expects them to comply without flinching. And oftentimes, he answers a question with a question, leaving his students feeling profoundly confused and frustrated.

Yet despite these methods – or more accurately, because of them – his students eventually got it. Jesus pushed the disciples to dig deeper, think harder, look further. And in their struggle to understand, they discovered truth and found faith in its Author. That's pretty powerful teaching.

Ted Swartz and Lee Eshleman understand this. Their dramatic portrayals of Peter and Andrew reveal what it must have been like to be the first students of the Teacher: the struggles, mystery, confusion, disappointment, failure, frustration, hunger, excitement, humor, joy and hope encountered on the journey to know Jesus and his plans for them. Like Jesus himself, Ted and Lee let us squirm and struggle to discover the truth.

The lessons in this book stay true to this method. No topical titles, no step-by-step approach to a clear message. Just encounters with Jesus and his disciples – via Ted and Lee's portrayals and the biblical accounts themselves – and some exercises to help students grapple with what Jesus' teachings mean for them in the here and now.

If this method is unfamiliar to your group, you may encounter some questions as you teach:

What's the point? Students who have been told the point or topic of every lesson have a difficult time discovering it for themselves. So answer this question before it gets asked: "I'm not going to tell you the point of this lesson – it's up to you to tell *me.*"

What if we miss the point? The trouble with letting students discover the point of a lesson is that they may miss what's most important, get sidetracked, or misinterpret it altogether. Welcome to Jesus' world: The disciples often missed his points too. So respond as Jesus did. Ask more questions, seek clarification, challenge their reasoning. Jesus' own very-great-great-great step-grandfather Sol put it this way:

> *My son, if you accept my words and store up my commands*
> *within you, turning your ear to wisdom and applying your heart to*
> *understanding, and if you call out for insight and cry aloud for*
> *understanding, and if you look for it as for silver and search for it as*
> *for hidden treasure, then you will understand the fear of the LORD*
> *and find the knowledge of God.*

—Proverb 2:1-5 (NIV)

What if I don't get it either? While you may be a teacher to your students, you're still a student of the Teacher. So do your homework before you teach: What is Jesus telling you personally? If it's difficult to comprehend, believe or act upon, why? Because when it comes down to it, if you haven't grappled with the lesson personally, your teaching will lack authority and authenticity anyway.

What if there's no single clear point? If you've been a student of Jesus for a while, you've discovered this fact: There seldom is. Each student is in a different place in his or her faith journey. The critical point of a lesson for one student may have little meaning to another at that moment in time. Not to worry: The Teacher who taught these lessons long ago is alive and at work today. If we let him, he'll draw each of us to what's most important for us to know and act on right now.

You might also prepare yourself for this question: *Why do the actors' portrayals differ from the gospel accounts?* No doubt about it, Ted and Lee add things to the stories, leave out others, and get some of the details wrong. If you treat their portrayals like scenes from the *Jesus* film, you'll be disappointed. But literal visualization is not their intent. They've provided us with comedic glimpses of the disciples that reveal what they're thinking and feeling – not play-by-play accounts of what actually happened. So use them as they were intended: Show a clip to help students identify with the disciples. Then use the gospel account to see what really happened.

Todd Temple

For almost a decade, and hundreds upon hundreds of shows, we have been pulling Simon Peter and his brother Andrew off the pages of scripture and onto the stage, as very human characters in the greatest of all stories.

After performances, people often ask us: "Where'd you get the idea to do this?" Sometimes an elderly person will remark, "You know, in all my years of studying the Bible, I never really thought of the disciples as human before. What led you to play them this way?" Or from a teenager: "Dude! [We hope they never stop calling us that] That was really funny! Where'd you get the idea to do that?"

The answer to all these questions is, of course: "yeast." In some translations of Mark 8, it says the disciples "huddled together" to discuss what Jesus meant by "yeast of the Pharisees." That image – funny, compelling, arresting in its simplicity – is rather striking: It suggests that Peter and Andrew weren't saints, carrying around all the answers. They were human. They were, at times, confused. They huddled.

From that first image, part of a monologue Ted wrote in seminary, to the co-written play that we authored three years later, we kept seeing how important it is that Jesus picked very simple men to be his first friends. And we kept seeing things that made us laugh the "aha" laugh. The laugh that is, perhaps, a way of hearing grace.

So, we present these scenes, encounters with Jesus: an Insider's View. Perhaps you already know these stories. If so, we invite you to take a fresh look and perhaps find yourself in them in a new way. And if they are new to you, welcome; you are about to discover stories that, after two thousand-odd years still continue to surprise and change us.

Many of you are reading this because you've agreed to teach a class or lead a Bible study with young folks. For that we thank you and offer our belief that kids gravitate toward what is true and what is funny. It is our sincere hope that these portrayals of Peter and Andrew show that the gospel story is both. And much more. So, huddle around. We've got some stories to tell.

Ted Swartz
Lee Eshleman

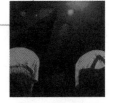

Fish Tales

Lesson One

passage: Luke 5:1-7

Teacher to Teacher

Watch the video clip, then read the passage and continue through verse 11. Ask Jesus to show you what's most important for you to deal with here. A few questions to ponder: What did you think of Jesus before you actually met him? What did your picture of him look like? What did he do that caused this picture to change?

In the video Andrew refers to a not spot: "A spot where the fish are not … is a not spot." While the scene in the video ends before the brothers return to that spot, the passage reveals what happens when they do: The not spot becomes a hot spot — Pete and Andy catch more fish than their net and boat can handle.

Jesus seems to revel in turning not spots to hot spots. Can you think of a time when he did this in your own life — turning an empty, fruitless or hopeless situation into one of overflowing blessing? If so, why do you suppose he did it? What was he trying to teach you about himself?

Source Notes

The Lake of Gennesaret and Sea of Galilee are one and the same. The lake is located about 70 miles north of Jerusalem, 13 miles long, eight miles wide, and surrounded by hills. The runoff from the lake forms the Jordan River, which in turn flows into the Dead Sea.

By the way, Simon receives his nickname Peter from Jesus later in the story (see Matthew 16:18), but the gospel writers refer to him as Simon or Peter or Simon Peter throughout their accounts, since they wrote them in retrospect.

Clip Notes

Fish Tales (Clip 1): Two frustrated fishermen, brothers Pete (played by Ted Swartz) and Andy (Lee Eshleman), are mending their nets after an unsuccessful fishing expedition. They're approached by someone who gives them unsolicited fishing advice.

Note that Ted and Lee finish this scene before the guys take the fishing advice; the results are revealed in the passage. It's also worth mentioning that in this scene they appear not to know that the stranger is Jesus. As we'll explore in Lesson 12, even after spending years with Jesus, the two had trouble recognizing him in a scene similar to this one (see John 21:1-6). Ted and Lee's portrayal may be considered a composite view.

lesson outline

*If you fish, tell your saddest fish tale – perhaps a time when you tried
all day and caught nothing ... how your hopes and plans turned to naught ...
whether you doubted your abilities ... or thought you were being punished for
something you did wrong. If you don't fish, chances are you've got a good story
about why you don't. Perhaps you failed it as a kid ... or got grossed out by the
bait or the cleaning ... or had to get a tetanus shot after someone else's cast
embedded the hook in your in your ear.*

Segue:

> Pete and Andy are brothers and partners in a fishing business, and they
> have a sad fish tale too.

the clip

Show Clip 1, Fish Tales, then invite students to react to what they've just seen:

What are your impressions of the characters? How would you
describe their personalities?

What kind of mood are they in? Why?

What's their initial reaction to the stranger and his fishing advice?
Why?

If you had been fishing all day and caught nothing, and someone
approached you with fishing advice, how would you react?

Why is it tough for most of us to take advice from others?

Why do you suppose Pete and Andy changed their minds and
decided to follow the advice?

Read Luke 5:1-7, point out that Simon and Peter are one and the same, then discuss the passage:

How does the real story differ from the scene in the video?

What do you suppose Peter and Andrew think of Jesus as they're heading out to deep water to try again?

What might they be thinking and feeling about Jesus as they're hauling in the huge catch?

How do you think they'd feel if they pulled in an empty net, even after doing what Jesus said?

Why do you suppose Jesus did this cool thing for these frustrated fisherman? What was the point of it all?

Pretend for a moment that all you know about Jesus is just what you've witnessed in this scene: What do you think of Jesus – who is he, what does he do, what's his personality?

How does this make you feel toward him?

Repeat Andy's line in the video where he talks about the "not spot" – "a spot where the fish are not … is a not spot." Then tell the group about a "not spot" in your own life that Jesus turned into a hot spot … or perhaps a condition that Jesus hasn't yet transformed. Share what you've learned, or are learning, about Jesus because of this situation. Then invite students to reflect on their own "not spots":

Can you recall a time when you had given up hope of changing a situation, and Jesus showed up and changed it radically? (Ask a few students to share their stories with the group.)

Do you have a "not spot" in your life right now? What would happen if Jesus showed up and told you to cast your net there again?

How would the situation be different? How would your life be different? How would your picture of Jesus change as a result? (You might ask a couple students to share their thoughts here, or simply ask them to reflect personally on them.)

Jesus is the teacher, you're his student: What's the Teacher want you to know from this fishing lesson? And what difference will that make in your life this week?

One day as Jesus was standing by the Lake of Gennesaret, with the people crowding around him and listening to the word of God, he saw at the water's edge two boats, left there by the fishermen, who were washing their nets. He got into one of the boats, the one belonging to Simon, and asked him to put out a little from shore. Then he sat down and taught the people from the boat. When he had finished speaking, he said to Simon, "Put out into deep water, and let down the nets for a catch." Simon answered, "Master, we've worked hard all night and haven't caught anything. But because you say so, I will let down the nets." When they had done so, they caught such a large number of fish that their nets began to break. So they signaled their partners in the other boat to come and help them, and they came and filled both boats so full that they began to sink.

—Luke 5:1-7 (NIV)

Fine Wine

Lesson TWO

passage: John 2:1-11

Teacher to Teacher

The best (and only) way to prepare for this lesson is to take it yourself. Watch the video, pray, read the passage, answer the suggested questions in the outline. Let Jesus show you what he wants you to know about himself, and what that means for you today.

Source Notes

A Jewish wedding is a big affair. The whole community shows up for the party, which is held at the house of the groom or his parents. This demands lots of food and wine. At this particular wedding, the groom runs out of the latter – not a good thing. Jesus' mom coaxes her son to save the day.

Jesus does it big-time. All told, he creates about 150 gallons – the equivalent of about 760 bottles. Let's see ... at $40 a bottle for fine wine, this wedding gift would be worth over $30,000 today.

Clip Notes

Fine Wine (Clip 2): There are actually two scenes here. In the first, Pete and Andy are in a receiving line, speaking with the wedding party and recounting the remarkable catch they hauled in after following Jesus' advice (in the previous lesson). In the second scene the two witness the results of Jesus' miracle with the wine.

Ted and Lee give us a refreshing view of this episode in the disciples' lives. While John with benefit of retrospect gives us a summary of the miracle at the wedding, the actors portray it from a more distant and colorful vantage point. It's not hard to imagine that in all the festivities Pete and Andy could have been less than attentive to Jesus' doings, and therefore caught by surprise when they tasted the results.

lesson outline

prologue

You might open the lesson with a quick story about something funny or unusual you witnessed at a wedding, then ask a couple students to share their own tales of unusual wedding episodes.

Segue:

> Early in their careers with Jesus, the disciples attended a wedding where Jesus did something very strange. Let's watch Pete and Andy's reactions to it.

the clip

Show Clip 2, Fine Wine, then invite students to react to what they've just seen:

> Describe Pete and Andy as portrayed by Ted and Lee. What kind of people are they?

> How are they feeling at the wedding reception? Awkward, excited, proud, embarrassed? Why?

> If you asked them to describe Jesus *before* they saw the wine miracle, what would they say?

> What would they say about Jesus *after* witnessing the miracle?

the source

Read John 2:1-11, then discuss the passage:

> Jesus tells his mom he doesn't want to do this miracle. Why?

> But then he goes and does the miracle anyway. Why do you think he relents?

> Besides saving the wedding host from embarrassment and allowing the party to carry on, what effect do you think this miracle has on the people there?

John, who recorded this wedding episode, writes near the end of this book, "Jesus did many other things as well. If every one of them were written down, I suppose that even the whole world would not have room for the books that would be written" (John 21:25). Which makes you wonder: Why did John include *this* episode? What's he want us to know about Jesus?

the next step

Invite students to pretend for a moment that they are at this wedding alongside the other disciples and talk about what they're seeing, thinking, feeling:

Jesus *could* have chosen not to perform this miracle. He also could have chosen to keep it a secret. Instead, he lets you catch him in the act of turning plain old water into top-quality wine. Why does he let you see this miracle?

What's he want you to know about him right now?

Does knowing Jesus in this way change your relationship with him? How?

Share your own thoughts on what Jesus is showing you in this episode — and how this new perspective might change how you think and act this week.

Your turn. What might you think or do differently this week because of what you now know about Jesus from this episode?

On the third day a wedding took place at Cana in Galilee. Jesus' mother was there, and Jesus and his disciples had also been invited to the wedding. When the wine was gone, Jesus' mother said to him, "They have no more wine." "Dear woman, why do you involve me?" Jesus replied. "My time has not yet come." His mother said to the servants, "Do whatever he tells you." Nearby stood six stone water jars, the kind used by the Jews for ceremonial washing, each holding from twenty to thirty gallons. Jesus said to the servants, "Fill the jars with water"; so they filled them to the brim. Then he told them, "Now draw some out and take it to the master of the banquet." They did so, and the master of the banquet tasted the water that had been turned into wine. He did not realize where it had come from, though the servants who had drawn the water knew. Then he called the bridegroom aside and said, "Everyone brings out the choice wine first and then the cheaper wine after the guests have had too much to drink; but you have saved the best till now." This, the first of his miraculous signs, Jesus performed at Cana in Galilee. He thus revealed his glory, and his disciples put their faith in him.

—John 2:1-11 (NIV)

Sermon Notes

Lesson **Three**

passage: Matthew 5-7

Teacher to Teacher

Take the lesson yourself, reading the entire sermon (Matthew 5-7) – yes, the whole thing. Ask Jesus to show you what's most important for you here, and how you might share that with your students.

Note that this lesson departs from the structure used in most of the others in that there's a visit to the gospel account before the video is shown. Since the characters in the clip are reflecting on the sermon they've already heard, it makes sense to let students experience it first, then catch Pete and Andy as they look back on it too.

Source Notes

While Jesus' miracles never fail to grab the public's attention, it's his remarkable teaching that keeps hold of that attention. In this his most famous sermon, he breaks nearly every homiletics rule in the book, hitting several big topics and touching on dozens of smaller ones.

Clip Notes

Sermon Notes (Clip 3): Pete and Andy reflect on the big sermon Jesus had given earlier. They wrestle with what's important about it, come up with some confusing instructions, then settle on the part that seems to convey the whole point of it: The Lord's Prayer.

Ted and Lee give us what's the most realistic take on this sermon since it was first preached. They don't show us the message itself, but what they took from it. At first Pete and Andy struggle to remember Jesus' extensive teachings, figuring that if they memorize it all, they'll do well on some big test to come.

But in the end they seem to grasp Jesus' real message here: It's not about memorizing the facts and figures, or flogging themselves into obedience over a long list of seemingly impossible rules. It's about discovering that the King has come, bringing with him not a new set of rules, but a way of living that flows from the inside out. In short, it's more about being than doing.

lesson outline

Read the following list to the group after asking, "What do these things have in common?"

- Blessed are the poor in spirit.
- You are the salt of the earth.
- A city on a hill cannot be hidden.
- If your right hand causes you to sin, cut it off.
- Love your enemies.
- Give in secret.
- Give us today our daily bread.
- Don't store up treasures on earth.
- You cannot serve both God and Money.
- Do not worry about tomorrow.
- Do not judge, or you too will be judged.
- Pull the plank out of your own eye.
- Seek and you will find.
- Enter through the narrow gate.
- Watch out for false prophets.
- A good tree cannot bear bad fruit.

Let students take some guesses. The best answer, of course, is, "things Jesus preaches in the Sermon on the Mount." Then ask students to break into seven groups. Give each its own section of the sermon. Each group is to read its passage together and come up with a summary or theme statement for it. Give the groups about four to five minutes for this activity. Here are the sermon sections. (Tip: If you have lots of students, feel free to subdivide the passages to form more groups, or give two or more groups the same passage.)

1. Matthew 5:3-12
2. Matthew 5:13-30
3. Matthew 5:31-48
4. Matthew 6:1-15
5. Matthew 6:16-34
6. Matthew 7:1-14
7. Matthew 7:15-27

When the small groups have completed their tasks, invite someone from each group to share their summary statement. It's helpful if you can write these statements on the board. When you have statements for each of the sermon's sections, ask students to brainstorm a title or summary statement for the entire sermon. Write these down too.

Segue:

No doubt about it – Jesus covers a lot of topics in this one sermon. It's tough enough to summarize each section; coming up with a summary or title for the whole message is really hard. Let's see how Ted & Lee's characters – the disciples Pete and Andy – do after they hear Jesus' most famous sermon.

the clip

Show Clip 3, Sermon Notes, then invite students to react to what they've just seen:

What do you suppose Pete and Andy think of Jesus' sermon? How do they feel about it?

Why are they trying to memorize his message?

Do you think they understand it all? Why or why not?

Based on this scene, what do you suppose they would say is the most important point or theme of the message?

the source

Read Matthew 6:9-13 (the Lord's Prayer), then discuss the passage:

After all the other sections we've summarized in this sermon, does it seem that Jesus' prayer is an oversimplification of everything we're supposed to be and do? Why or why not?

What does Jesus mean by "your kingdom come"? Is he praying for God's kingdom to come, or has it already arrived?

If the kingdom has arrived, who brought it? Who's the king?

What else in this prayer do you think is important?

Looking back on the video, why would Pete and Andy remember this prayer above everything else Jesus said?

the next step

In his sermon, Jesus quotes the "old masters" – things the great writers of the Old Testament said that the people were supposed to do – but he puts a "new spin" on them. What's this new spin? How does Jesus' message differ from theirs?

In most cases, it seems like Jesus' "rules" for these things – giving, loving, marriage, etc. – are even *more* difficult to obey. Why do you suppose he makes things more difficult, not less?

If living up to Jesus' standards on these things is so difficult, what hope do we have of obeying? Where does Jesus fit in?

What's that mean for you today? Are you trying to do Christian things instead of living in Jesus first? If you make the *being* part the first thing, what happens to the *doing* part?

> This, then, is how you should pray: "'Our Father in heaven, hallowed be your name, your kingdom come, your will be done on earth as it is in heaven. Give us today our daily bread. Forgive us our debts, as we also have forgiven our debtors. And lead us not into temptation, but deliver us from the evil one.'
>
> —Matt 6:9-13 (NIV)

Fast Food

Lesson Four

passage: Matthew 14:14-22

Teacher to Teacher

Take the lesson yourself: Watch the video, react to it, then read the passage and reflect on the discussion questions that follow. Pay special attention to the "deeper" questions: Be ready to share examples from your own life of how you obeyed Jesus in something that seemed silly, pointless or impossible, only to see him step in and provide the part that only he could give – the part that turned the experience into a miracle.

Source Notes

Some of us city dwellers have a tough time appreciating the situation the disciples are concerned about. In our world there always seems to be a fast-food joint or 7-11 down the street, ready to answer the call of a grumbling stomach. But this scene takes place in the country: The disciples have several thousand hungry people on their hands and not a Denny's in sight. Their solution – to send the folks home to dinner – is a good one. But Jesus has a better idea.

Clip Notes

Fast Food (Clip 4): Pete and Andy are worried about the hungry crowd and suggest to Jesus that he send them home for dinner. Jesus has a different solution. The two disciples follow his plan, first with doubt, then with amazement.

It's a real treat to watch Ted and Lee perform this piece live. They return from the audience with their arms full of every snack imaginable, along with

a wide assortment of gum and breath mints. Which makes the scene come to life: In any crowd you're going to find food stuffed into backpacks and pockets and purses. The owners of that food might be taking secret bites ... and feeling guilty because they don't have enough to share. It's not hard to imagine such conditions in the original scene. Jesus knows there's some food out there; the miracle is in turning it into a full-blown meal for everyone.

It's worth noting that in the clip, Pete and Andy struggle to find the "deeper meaning" of the miracle. While this particular Bible passage doesn't include this dialog, many others reveal that the disciples struggle to comprehend much of what Jesus is saying and doing; sometimes they ask their Teacher, sometimes they don't (see Matthew 13:36, Luke 8:25; 9:45).

Indeed, regarding this very miracle, Mark writes, "for they had not understood about the loaves; their hearts were hardened" (6:52).

lesson outline

Briefly tell of a time when you attended a big event where food was not provided or wasn't easy to get to: long lines at the snack bar, exorbitant prices, whatever. Describe how you felt, how it was difficult to listen on an empty stomach, how you coveted the Tootsie Roll of the person next to you, etc.

Segue:

> The disciples are at an event like that. They're in the middle of nowhere with Jesus and a crowd of several thousand hungry people. There are no snack bars, no restaurants nearby. It's dinner time and someone needs to do something.

the clip

Show Clip 4, Fast Food, then invite students to react to what they've just seen:

> How do you suppose Pete and Andy are feeling at the start of this episode?

> Do you think they act the way disciples should act? How so or not?

> Why do you think they're afraid to talk to Jesus?

> Why do they have such trouble understanding him?

> How do you feel when you don't understand something Jesus has said or done? What do you do in response to this feeling?

the source

Read Matthew 14:14-22 and discuss the passage:

> What elements in the video clip aren't recorded in the passage?

> What things in the passage aren't in the clip?

Why do you suppose Jesus performs this miracle? Who are the beneficiaries? Who benefits most?

What do you suppose the disciples think of Jesus after witnessing this miracle? What's their picture of Jesus look like?

Unlike when Jesus transforms the water to wine at the wedding, for this miracle he gets the disciples to help. Why do you think he does it this way?

the next step

You've heard the expression, "God helps those who ... (help themselves)." Despite what people say, you won't find this statement anywhere in the Bible. But is it true nonetheless? How does it compare with what happens in this episode? (note: The disciples don't initiate things here – they're following Jesus' instructions.)

If you can, think of a time when you sensed Jesus telling you to do something embarrassing or stupid or impossible, and you did it anyway. Did he step in and complete the work so that it turned out OK? (note: Briefly tell a personal example here, then invite a couple students to tell their own.)

How about now? Has he asked you to do something that you're afraid to try? What would happen if you did it? Would he come through with his part? How would your life be different? How would your picture of Jesus be different?

What message does Jesus have for you in this lesson? What's he want you to know or do in response to it?

> When Jesus landed and saw a large crowd, he had compassion on them and healed their sick. As evening approached, the disciples came to him and said, "This is a remote place, and it's already getting late. Send the crowds away, so they can go to the villages and buy themselves some food." Jesus replied, "They do not need to go away. You give them something to eat." "We have here only five loaves of bread and two fish," they answered. "Bring them here to me," he said. And he directed the people to sit down on the grass. Taking the five loaves and the two fish and looking up to heaven, he gave thanks and broke the loaves. Then he gave them to the disciples, and the disciples gave them to the people. They all ate and were satisfied, and the disciples picked up twelve basketfuls of broken pieces that were left over. The number of those who ate was about five thousand men, besides women and children. Immediately Jesus made the disciples get into the boat and go on ahead of him to the other side, while he dismissed the crowd.
> —Matthew 14:14-22 (NIV)

Sea Stroll

Lesson **Five**

passage: Matthew 14:23-33

Teacher to Teacher

Read the passage and ask God to reveal to you a fresh perspective from it. Reflect on times when you attempted gutsy acts because of your faith. What was the outcome? Write down something you did that you know was right but you were ridiculed for it.

Source Notes

This episode takes place on the Lake of Gennesaret, or Sea of Galilee. As fishermen, Peter and Andrew (along with the other pair of brother disciples, James and John) know the lake well. It's likely that they've spent many a night on it, netting catches to sell the next morning. After the miraculous feeding of several thousand people earlier that evening, Jesus sends the disciples out on the lake while he stays ashore to pray. Between three and six o'clock in the morning ("the fourth watch") he rejoins them, getting there on his own two feet.

Clip Notes

Sea Stroll (Clip 5): Following orders but not knowing why, Pete and Andy row out onto the Sea of Galilee, leaving Jesus ashore. Jesus catches up to them in the midst of a storm, and the two disciples react in fear, faith, and amazement.

If you're familiar with Matthew's account of Jesus' walk on the water, you may notice that Ted and Lee leave out two of Peter's lines. The first is his asking Jesus to bid him out onto the lake himself as proof of Jesus' identity; the second is his call to Jesus for help when he starts to sink. If you feel that these are essential to the story, you can call attention to them in the discussion following the reading of the passage. However, you might also note that

Matthew's gospel is the only account in which Peter has any lines at all. Mark and John keep Peter frightened but dry onboard, while Luke leaves out the episode altogether.

lesson outline

To open the lesson you might briefly share a personal story about nearly drowning, or some other near-death experience, and how you lived to tell about it. If you don't have such a tale to tell, chances are someone else in the group does: Ask him or her to share the story.

Segue:

> Jesus and the disciples have just fed a crowd of several thousand people on the shore of the Sea of Galilee, thanks to Jesus' miracle of turning a few loaves and some fish into a feast.

the clip

Show Clip 5, Sea Stroll, then invite students to react to what they've just seen:

Why do you suppose Pete says, "I just do what I'm told"?

What kinds of things might the disciples be feeling as they get in the boat?

How would you react if you saw someone standing in the middle of a lake? What would you be thinking and feeling?

What do you think moves Pete to step out of the boat? Why does Andy stay in?

the source

Read Matthew 14:23-33 and discuss the passage:

How does this scene as portrayed in the video differ from the real story?

Why does Jesus send the disciples out on the lake without him?

Does Peter really walk on the water?

Why does he start to sink?

What keeps him from drowning?

What do you suppose Peter is thinking and feeling when he gets back in the boat?

How about the other disciples? What might they be thinking and feeling?

the next step

Most of us tend to look at Peter in this episode in one of two ways: We either focus on his failure – after all, he needed to be rescued – or we focus on the fact that he actually walked on water for a few steps. How do you tend to look at the mixed results of your own bold steps in faith? Do you dwell on the failure, or are you able to rejoice in the successes? Why do you give one side more attention than the other?

Can you think of a time in your own life when you stepped boldly in faith, got into trouble, and Jesus rescued you? *(Invite a couple of students to share their stories here; make it safe by telling your story first.)*

How about a time when he *didn't* rescue you? Why didn't he? *(Again, go first with your own story, then ask for a couple from students.)*

What's Jesus' lesson to *you* in this story? What's he want you to know, feel, do?

Can you think of a "bold step of faith" you might take this week? What is it? When would you do it? What might happen if you did? How might you fail? How might Jesus rescue you if you did? What would happen if he didn't? Is it worth the risk?

After he had dismissed them, he went up on a mountainside by himself to pray. When evening came, he was there alone, but the boat was already a considerable distance from land, buffeted by the waves because the wind was against it. During the fourth watch of the night Jesus went out to them, walking on the lake. When the disciples saw him walking on the lake, they were terrified. "It's a ghost," they said, and cried out in fear. But Jesus immediately said to them: "Take courage! It is I. Don't be afraid." "Lord, if it's you," Peter replied, "tell me to come to you on the water." "Come," he said. Then Peter got down out of the boat, walked on the water and came toward Jesus. But when he saw the wind, he was afraid and, beginning to sink, cried out, "Lord, save me!" Immediately Jesus reached out his hand and caught him. "You of little faith," he said, "why did you doubt?" And when they climbed into the boat, the wind died down. Then those who were in the boat worshiped him, saying, "Truly you are the Son of God."

—Matthew 14:23-33 (NIV)

Mountain Morph

Lesson Six

passage: Matthew 17:1-9

Teacher to Teacher

Take the lesson on your own: watch the video, answer the questions that follow it. Then read the passage, reflect on the discussion questions. Ask Jesus to show you what's most important for you here.

Source Notes

This lesson's passage covers the transfiguration scene: Jesus takes his three closest disciples, Peter, James and John, up a high mountain in the Galilee region (Mount Hermon seems likely, but the gospel writers don't tell us) to witness an amazing event. They see their Teacher's glory unveiled in company with Moses and Elijah, who had had their own encounters with the Almighty on another mountain (Sinai) long ago. And like those old heroes, they hear the voice of God, who makes it clear that Jesus is his son, and therefore greater than all others.

Clip Notes

Mountain Morph (Clip 6): Pete, frustrated by misunderstanding Jesus yet again, is packing his bag. He's quitting the disciple team. With no small degree of embarrassment he tells Andy what happened when he saw Moses and Elijah show up. When his brother reminds him of the other amazing things that have happened in Jesus' midst, Pete starts unpacking. Like the clip in Lesson 3, in which the brothers recall the Sermon on the Mount, this clip's scene isn't found in the gospels. In this case, Ted and Lee use the siblings' conversation to recount the transfiguration scene – and to touch on other great episodes in their adventures with Jesus.

In one sense it seems unlikely that Peter would want to quit the team after witnessing such an unambiguous affirmation of Jesus' greatness. But then again, haven't we all had that same feeling at one point or another in our faith journey? Mountain-top certainties turn foggy in life's valleys; the thrill of being rescued by Jesus gives way to the realities of living under his lordship.

Perhaps most powerful in this clip is the actors' depiction of the frustration, confusion and embarrassment the disciples must have felt as they tried to make sense of their teachers' outlandish lessons – something we modern disciples can surely relate to.

lesson outline

If you have such a story, briefly tell of a time when a "spiritual mountaintop" experience was all too soon replaced by discouragement, doubt, or a return to your old ways. Alternatively, you might tell of a time when you contemplated or actually threw in the towel and gave up on your faith. In either case, share what you thought about Jesus at the time, and how you felt about yourself.

the clip

Show Clip 6, Mountain Morph, then invite students to react to what they've just seen:

How do you think Pete feels as this scene opens? Why might he be feeling this way?

What's Andrew feeling? Why?

What does Andrew do in response to his big brother's doubts? Why? Is his a good strategy?

In the end, why do you suppose Pete reconsiders?

the source

Read Matthew 17:1-9, then discuss the passage:

Why do you suppose Moses and Elijah show up in this scene?

What's Peter's response – and why do you think he gives it?

Why do you suppose Jesus takes just three of the 12 disciples with him for this event?

What does he want them to know about himself?

Why does he tell them to keep quiet about what they've seen?

the next step

Think of a time when Jesus revealed himself to you in a big way. How did he do it? How did it change your view of Jesus at the time? (Tip: Make it safe by being the first to share here.)

Did this view fade afterward? Why?

Think of a time when you had serious doubts about your ability to remain a disciple of Jesus – perhaps a time when you were ready to give up your faith. What led you to this low spot? Why did you doubt?

What brought you back? Why did you not give up ... or if you did, why did you return?

If Jesus were to reveal himself in your circumstances this week – in a way that would further assure you of his love, power, forgiveness, whatever – how would he do it? How would you know it was he? How would this change your faith?

> After six days Jesus took with him Peter, James and John the brother of James, and led them up a high mountain by themselves. There he was transfigured before them. His face shone like the sun, and his clothes became as white as the light. Just then there appeared before them Moses and Elijah, talking with Jesus. Peter said to Jesus, "Lord, it is good for us to be here. If you wish, I will put up three shelters— one for you, one for Moses and one for Elijah." While he was still speaking, a bright cloud enveloped them, and a voice from the cloud said, "This is my Son, whom I love; with him I am well pleased. Listen to him!" When the disciples heard this, they fell facedown to the ground, terrified. But Jesus came and touched them. "Get up," he said. "Don't be afraid." When they looked up, they saw no one except Jesus. As they were coming down the mountain, Jesus instructed them, "Don't tell anyone what you have seen, until the Son of Man has been raised from the dead."
>
> —Matthew 17:1-9 (NIV)

Palm Parade

Lesson **Seven**

passage: Matthew 21:1-11

Teacher to Teacher

Watch the video and read the passage. Ask yourself when you thought your ministry was at its peak in popularity and acclaim. Why do you think so? In retrospect, was this popularity about God or was it about you?

Source Notes

In fulfillment of an Old Testament forecast, Jesus enters Jerusalem on the back of a donkey, to the delight of his followers and the amazement of the crowds. He gets the "red carpet" treatment – the dust and mud before him paved in branches and cloaks.

We now remember this great day as Palm Sunday – the first day in the week leading up to his death and resurrection.

Clip Notes

Palm Parade (Clip 7): Pete and Andy, celebrities in the palm parade, bask in the glory of their discipleship status ... and wonder what the future will bring.

As with a few other scenes in this series, Ted and Lee give us a view of a biblical event from a vantage point not recorded in the Bible. In this case we see Jesus' entrance parade not as spectators but as participants. Having struggled and stumbled their way through discipleship class, Pete and Andy now seem rather sure of their stature. They finally get it. Or do they? All the excitement of the moment can't dispel their fears about how this class will end.

lesson outline

prologue

Play a quick game of Brush with Fame: *Ask students if they've ever met some-one famous ... or at least gotten within a few feet of someone famous. Invite a few students to briefly tell their stories, then ask them how this moment made them feel – and how the celebrity seemed to feel about it.*

Segue:

> In this next clip, Pete and Andy are celebrities – members of Jesus' exclu-sive disciple team making their big entrance into Jerusalem with their now famous Teacher. Let's see how they handle their new-found fame.

the clip

Show Clip 7, Palm Parade, *then invite students to react to what they've just seen:*

> How do you think Pete and Andy are feeling at this moment? What evidence can you cite?
>
> Are they acting the way you'd expect Jesus' disciples to act?
>
> If you were in their place, how would you act?
>
> Why do you suppose they're a bit apprehensive about the future?

the source

Read Matthew 21:1-11, then discuss the passage:

> How does the actors' portrayal of this scene differ from the gospel account? What do Ted and Lee add to the story, and what have they left out?
>
> Why does Jesus ask for a donkey? How does he know it will be there waiting for him just as he describes?

Why do you think the crowd lays down cloaks and branches?

Why do you suppose the crowd is so enthusiastic about Jesus' entrance? What are they thinking will happen after he arrives?

What do you suppose Jesus is thinking at this moment?

the next step

If you were a spectator at this parade, hearing about seeing Jesus for the first time, what would you think of him? What kind of person is he?

Does Jesus receive this kind of praise today? Why or why not?

Looking at your own life right now, where are you in this parade? Are you in his disciple entourage, basking in the limelight, like Pete and Andy in the video? Or in the crowd, praising Jesus? Or perhaps standing back and wondering what all the excitement is about? Why have you chosen this place? *(Tip: Go first by answering this question yourself.)*

Here's a tough one: At one extreme, you'll find people who join in the praises of Jesus – in church, in worship, in Christian events – only because that's what the crowd is doing; they're there for all the excitement. At the other extreme you'll find folks who would celebrate Jesus if they were the only one who showed up. Most of us fall somewhere between these two extremes.

Honestly, where do you think you are in this continuum? How much of your enthusiasm for Jesus comes from the crowd, how much from your faith in Jesus himself? *(Again, make it safe by answering first ... with total honesty.)*

If you applied his lesson this week, what would it look like?

As they approached Jerusalem and came to Bethphage on the Mount of Olives, Jesus sent two disciples, saying to them, "Go to the village ahead of you, and at once you will find a donkey tied there, with her colt by her. Untie them and bring them to me. If anyone says anything to you, tell him that the Lord needs them, and he will send them right away." This took place to fulfill what was spoken through the prophet: "Say to the Daughter of Zion, 'See, your king comes to you, gentle and riding on a donkey, on a colt, the foal of a donkey.'" The disciples went and did as Jesus had instructed them. They brought the donkey and the colt, placed their cloaks on them, and Jesus sat on them. A very large crowd spread their cloaks on the road, while others cut branches from the trees and spread them on the road. The crowds that went ahead of him and those that followed shouted, "Hosanna to the Son of David!" "Blessed is he who comes in the name of the Lord!" "Hosanna in the highest!" When Jesus entered Jerusalem, the whole city was stirred and asked, "Who is this?" The crowds answered, "This is Jesus, the prophet from Nazareth in Galilee."

—Matthew 21:1-11 (NIV)

Passover Plans

Lesson **Eight**

passage: Luke 22:7-13

Teacher to Teacher

Take the lesson yourself, watching the video clip, reading the passage, reflecting on the questions. Be prepared to share some of your answers with students to make the room safe for their own sharing.

Source Notes

The passage in this scene covers not the Last Supper itself, but the disciples' preparations for the meal. They've taken part in the Passover every year since they were born, in remembrance of the night long ago in Egypt when God's angel passed over every house whose doorway was marked in lamb's blood, slaying the first-born male in every house unmarked. On that night, lambs died to save God's children.

By Jesus' time, Passover has become a pilgrimage to Jerusalem. The streets are filled with out-of-towners, the markets stocked with year-old lambs and all the fixings for the traditional meal. But you won't find yeast on the shelves: When the Jews left Egypt, they did so in a hurry, carrying their unleavened dough with them. Which explains why Passover and the week that follows are sometimes called the Festival of Unleavened Bread.

Clip Notes

Passover Plans (Clip 8): Just arrived in the room where they'll be sharing Passover with Jesus, Pete and Andy make preparations for the meal.

Once again, Ted and Lee show us the disciples trying to make the best of a confusing situation. Andy has taken the liberty of drawing up how the scene will look when everyone's at the table – a seating arrangement that sounds remarkably like a description of Leonardo Da Vinci's famous Last Supper painting.

While some of the humor in this piece is subtle (and may be missed by those unfamiliar with the painting), the message here is even more so. Andy has a feeling that this meal will be significant, but doesn't quite know why. He repeats some of Jesus' veiled predictions of demise, but can't yet put them together. So, with no clear picture of the future, he makes the most of today. He's determined to be ready, just in case Jesus decides to do something big. A pretty good attitude for us too.

lesson outline

Open the lesson by asking students to describe what Jesus looks like: skin tone, facial features, color of eyes, color and style of hair, beard or no beard, halo or no halo, height, weight, posture, etc. Jot these down on the board – or better yet, recruit a student artist to draw a composite sketch as the group describes him.

Segue:

> The truth is, we have no sure picture of what Jesus looks like: If anyone sketched his portrait while he was on earth – and the art has survived somehow – archaeologists haven't found it yet. All we've got are artists' interpretations, painted several hundred years after Jesus' departure. But he's a real person, and in this next clip, the disciples are about to have a real meal with him. Andy has a feeling that this dinner will be something special. He's even drawn a sketch to show what it will look like when the Teacher and the rest of the students arrive and gather at the table. A class picture, more or less.

the clip

Show Clip 8, Passover Plans, then invite students to react to what they've just seen:

> Ted and Lee's characters are alluding to a classic painting. Any idea what it is and who painted it?
>
> What's Pete's mood in this scene? What's he feeling?
>
> What about Andy? What's he feeling – and why is he being so particular about the seating arrangements?
>
> Andy repeats a couple haunting lines they heard earlier from Jesus – one about tearing down the temple, another about the shepherd and his sheep – but neither of the guys know what they mean? What *do* they mean?
>
> Why do you suppose they don't understand the meaning of Jesus' words? Are they too mysterious to comprehend ... or are the guys

just stupid ... or perhaps they don't *want* to understand them?

the source

Read Luke 22:7-13, then discuss the passage:
What do Ted & Lee add to this scene that's not found in the passage?

What things do the actors leave out?

Why do you suppose Jesus uses the water guy to lead Peter and John to the proper room? Why doesn't he just give them a street address?

Do you think it's significant that Jesus schedules the meal in a room on an upper floor? What benefits might this provide?

Would the disciples think it strange that Jesus is making such a big deal out of this meal? How important is the Passover in general? What's special about this particular Passover?

the next step

Jesus' mysterious way of revealing the location of the room suggests that he's planning something important for this meal. The video clip does a good job of portraying the disciples' suspicions and apprehensions about this – and the worry and frustration of not knowing what it is. How do *you* feel when you suspect that something awful is going to happen to you, but don't know what it is? Why?

Jesus knows that he's about to be executed, and that he'll rise up from the grave afterward. He gives the disciples hints of this, but he doesn't ever come right out and tell them these things in plain and unambiguous words. Why not? How does this hurt or help the disciples? What would the disciples say about this?

In the same way, Jesus knows what's about to happen in *your* life. After all, he sees the future, including the awful stuff ahead. Why doesn't he tell it to you? How does this hurt or help you? If he doesn't come right out and tell you, does he do anything instead?

How do you feel about him for treating you this way?

Jesus sometimes gives us hints and clues to prepare us for what's ahead. What's he preparing *you* for right now? What clues do you have for this? What are you doing about them?

> Then came the day of Unleavened Bread on which the Passover lamb had to be sacrificed. Jesus sent Peter and John, saying, "Go and make preparations for us to eat the Passover." "Where do you want us to prepare for it?" they asked. He replied, "As you enter the city, a man carrying a jar of water will meet you. Follow him to the house that he enters, and say to the owner of the house, 'The Teacher asks: Where is the guest room, where I may eat the Passover with my disciples?' He will show you a large upper room, all furnished. Make preparations there." They left and found things just as Jesus had told them. So they prepared the Passover.
>
> —Luke 22:7-13 (NIV)

Clean Feet

Lesson **Nine**

passage: John 13:1-10

Teacher to Teacher

Take the lesson yourself and reflect on the questions. Ask Jesus to show you what's important here for you personally ... and what he wants your students to hear.

Note that this lesson includes a foot-washing as the opening illustration, so you'll want to prepare a basin, water, soap and towels for this. You might also want to conclude the lesson by having students wash each other's feet, in which case you'll need more of the same.

Source Notes
The passage is intimate. It shares Jesus' perspective and thoughts as well as the dismal reality that one of his close associates is about to be Satan's puppet and betray him to his enemies. Despite the circumstances, Jesus proceeds to undress before his friends and wash their feet. Peter objects, then submits as he understands the consequence of not allowing his Lord to carry out this act.

Clip Notes
Clean Feet (Clip 9): At first, Pete and Andy look like they're attending just another Passover meal. Then they begin to notice that this evening and what Jesus is saying and doing are somehow different — more important, even symbolic. The piece ends with one of these symbols.

lesson outline

prologue

For an opening illustration to this episode in the gospels, it's tough to beat a good old foot-washing. Get a volunteer to submit to your scrubbing, and while you're working, ask him or her how it feels to be the recipient of such treatment: Awkward, embarrassing? If the owner of the feet runs out of answers before you run out of feet, ask the rest of the group to talk about how they'd feel if they were up there instead.

Segue:

> Pete and Andy can relate to these feelings. After celebrating the Passover meal, their teacher gives them the clean-feet treatment.

the clip

Show Clip 9, Clean Feet, then invite students to react to what they've just seen:

> Pete and Andy seem to be figuring out that this is no ordinary Passover meal. What seems to be their first clue?
>
> What's Pete's reaction when he finds out Jesus wants to wash his feet? Why does he react this way?
>
> The disciples are picking up on the symbols Jesus gives them at this meal: What do you suppose they think the foot-washing means?
>
> What's the last thing the actors do in this scene – and what's it mean?

the source

Read John 13:1-10, then discuss the passages:

> What do Ted and Lee add to this scene that's not found in the passage?

What do you learn from the passage that's not in the video?

The passage says that Jesus "now showed them the full extent of his love." How does the foot-washing do that?

Why does Jesus strip down to just a towel to wash their feet? Is it just to keep his clothes dry, or is there something more to it?

When Peter asks Jesus what he's doing, Jesus tells Peter that it won't make sense now, but it will later. What's Jesus mean by this? Does it end up making sense for the disciples later? What would they say it meant?

What do you suppose the disciples think of Jesus after this experience? How might their picture of him have changed?

the next step

Jesus gets down on his knees and washes the dirtiest part of his disciples' bodies – they wear sandals and walk dusty, muddy streets – you get the picture. In what ways has Jesus washed you? How else has he served you?

How do these things demonstrate his love for you?

What's Jesus' lesson for you in this episode? Why does he let you catch him in the act of doing this humble thing?

How does he want you to respond? What would that look like this week?

It was just before the Passover Feast. Jesus knew that the time had come for him to leave this world and go to the Father. Having loved his own who were in the world, he now showed them the full extent of his love. The evening meal was being served, and the devil had already prompted Judas Iscariot, son of Simon, to betray Jesus. Jesus knew that the Father had put all things under his power, and that he had come from God and was returning to God; so he got up from the meal, took off his outer clothing, and wrapped a towel around his waist. After that, he poured water into a basin and began to wash his disciples' feet, drying them with the towel that was wrapped around him. He came to Simon Peter, who said to him, "Lord, are you going to wash my feet?" Jesus replied, "You do not realize now what I am doing, but later you will understand." "No," said Peter, "you shall never wash my feet." Jesus answered, "Unless I wash you, you have no part with me." "Then, Lord," Simon Peter replied, "not just my feet but my hands and my head as well!" Jesus answered, "A person who has had a bath needs only to wash his feet; his whole body is clean. And you are clean, though not every one of you."

–John 13:1-10 (NIV)

Twice Busted

Lesson **Ten**

passage: Matthew 26:47-58; 69-75

Teacher to Teacher

Take the lesson yourself. Pay special attention to Peter in the passages. How does his relationship with Jesus compare to yours? In what ways are you and Peter alike? How are you most different? What do you most admire about him? What don't you like?

Source Notes

The passage covers two scenes: The first is Jesus' arrest in the Garden of Gethsemane on the Mount of Olives. Gethsemane means olive press, suggesting that this garden was within an olive grove, where such a press would be found. Though the exact location of the garden is uncertain, the Mount of Olives upon which it existed is a short walk from the city center, across a valley to the east of the Temple site.

The second scene occurs at the home of Caiaphas, the high priest, where Jesus is taken to be interrogated and condemned by the Sanhedrin. This lesson skips verses 59-68 (the proceedings inside the home), jumping straight to Peter in the courtyard outside, where he denies his association with Jesus.

Clip Notes

Twice Busted (Clip 10): Like the passage, the clip contains two scenes: The hours just after Jesus' arrest, as Pete and Andy watch the soldiers haul Jesus away; Pete runs after the mob. In the second, Andy catches up to his brother in the courtyard outside the house where Jesus is being held.

Ted and Lee hit us hard with these two scenes: In the first, they set aside all humor to let us feel the disciples' fear and confusion. In the second, they juxtapose the humor with unsettling bursts of anger and sadness.

Ted's portrayal well conveys what Peter must have been feeling as he denied his Lord: a maddening sense of helplessness, an utter self-loathing.

lesson outline

You might open the lesson by briefly telling of a time when, in the fog of confusion or heat of anger, you did something very stupid, causing you great regret when your head cleared. Alternatively, tell of a time when you betrayed, denied or abandoned a friend in need, and how you felt about it afterward.

Segue:

After Jesus is arrested, Pete has a night like this. Let's see how he reacts as the soldiers haul his Teacher away:

the clip

Show Clip 10, Twice Busted, then invite students to react to what they've just seen:

What do you think Pete is feeling at the beginning of the clip as he watches the solider haul off Jesus? Why?

Andy holds his brother back: What are his feelings, and why do they differ from Pete's?

In the courtyard scene, why's Pete so afraid to be recognized? What do you think he fears might happen to him if he is?

When Pete says they've been lucky because no one but Jesus has been arrested yet, Andy replies, "I don't think luck has been a big factor in any of this." Finish his thought: What's he mean by this statement?

When asked for the third time whether he's part of Jesus' group, Pete explodes and starts cussing. Do you think that's how the real Peter acts at this moment? Why or why not?

Read Matthew 26:47-58 and 69-75, then discuss the passage:

What does the gospel account cover that's not in the video clip?

We know from other gospel accounts that the disciple who cuts off the soldier's ear is none other than Peter. Knowing that, and the other facts we've just read in the passage, does Pete's behavior in the clip make more sense? How or how not?

Peter is recognized three times by others in the courtyard. How do you suppose they know he's one of Jesus' disciples?

In the garden Peter is defending Jesus with a sword, alone against a gang of soldiers. In the courtyard later that same night he's afraid to tell even a servant girl that he's with Jesus. What do you suppose caused his actions to change so radically?

How do you think Peter feels the moment he hears the rooster's crowing?

What does his reaction tell you about his feelings for Jesus?

Of course, Jesus' story doesn't end here, nor does Peter's place on the disciple team. In fact, the two have a great reunion after Jesus returns from the grave. Since it all turns out so well, why does the Bible include this awful episode in Peter's life? Why didn't Peter tell the gospel writers to leave it out? Why did God allow it to stay in?

Peter's behavior in these scenes touches two extremes: In one he plays defending hero, in the other, a cursing coward. What would you think of someone today who calls himself a disciple of Jesus, yet behaves with such radical contradiction?

Take it personal: Can you think of a time when you passionately defended Jesus or your faith in him against opposition? What happened?

How about a time when you did the opposite – hiding in silence or denying him in words? Again, what happened – and how did you feel about it afterwards? *(Tip: Make this one safe by going first.)*

Pretend for a moment that Peter were here right now. The two of you go off and grab a Coke together and talk about your faith. What advice would he give you about how you treat Jesus?

If he said, "You know, there's this thing in your life right now that looks kind of like what I did that night in the courtyard," what would that thing be? Is there an area where fear or doubt, or confusion or frustration, is causing you to deny Jesus or push him away?

What would Peter tell you to do about it? How would your life and faith change as a result? What's preventing you from doing that this week?

While he was still speaking, Judas, one of the Twelve, arrived. With him was a large crowd armed with swords and clubs, sent from the chief priests and the elders of the people. Now the betrayer had arranged a signal with them: "The one I kiss is the man; arrest him." Going at once to Jesus, Judas said, "Greetings, Rabbi!" and kissed him. Jesus replied, "Friend, do what you came for." Then the men stepped forward, seized Jesus and arrested him. With that, one of Jesus' companions reached for his sword, drew it out and struck the servant of the high priest, cutting off his ear. "Put your sword back in its place," Jesus said to him, "for all who draw the sword will die by the sword. Do you think I cannot call on my Father, and he will at once put at my disposal more than twelve legions of angels? But how then would the Scriptures be fulfilled that say it must happen in this way?" At that time Jesus said to the crowd, "Am I leading a rebellion, that you have come out with swords and clubs to capture me? Every day I sat in the temple courts teaching, and you did not arrest me. But this has all taken place that the writings of the prophets might be fulfilled." Then all the disciples deserted him and fled. Those who had arrested Jesus took him to Caiaphas, the high priest, where the teachers of the law and the elders had assembled. But Peter followed him at a distance, right up to the courtyard of the high priest. He entered and sat down with the guards to see the outcome. The chief priests and the whole Sanhedrin were looking for false evidence against Jesus so that they could put him to death. But they did not find any, though many false witnesses came forward. Finally two came forward and declared, "This fellow said, 'I am able to destroy the temple of God and rebuild it in three days.'" Then the high priest stood up and said to Jesus, "Are you not going to answer? What is this testimony that these men are bringing against you?" But Jesus remained silent. The high priest said to him, "I charge you under oath by the living God: Tell us if you are the Christ, the Son of God." "Yes, it is as you say," Jesus replied. "But I say to all of you: In the future you will see the Son of Man sitting at the right hand of the Mighty One and coming on the clouds of heaven." Then the high priest tore his clothes and said, "He has spoken blasphemy! Why do we need any more witnesses? Look, now you have heard the blasphemy. What do you think?" "He is worthy of death," they answered. Then they spit in his face and struck him with their fists. Others slapped him and said, "Prophesy to us, Christ. Who hit you?" Now Peter was sitting out in the courtyard, and a servant girl came to him. "You also were with Jesus of Galilee," she said. But he denied it before them all. "I don't know what you're talking about," he said. Then he went out to the gateway, where another girl saw him and said to the people there, "This fellow was with Jesus of Nazareth." He denied it again, with an oath: "I don't know the man!" After a little while, those standing there went up to Peter and said, "Surely you are one of them, for your accent gives you away." Then he began to call down curses on himself and he swore to them, "I don't know the man!" Immediately a rooster crowed. Then Peter remembered the word Jesus had spoken: "Before the rooster crows, you will disown me three times." And he went outside and wept bitterly.

—Matt 26:47-75 (NIV)

Roomy Tomb

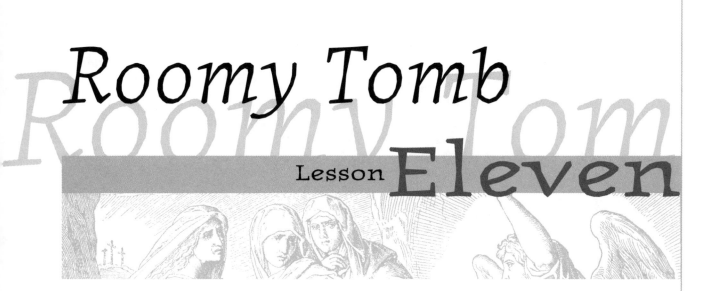

Lesson **Eleven**

passage: Luke 24:1-12

Teacher to Teacher

You know the drill: Take the lesson; reflect on what Jesus is telling you about himself and your life as his disciple ... and be ready to share what you've learned.

Source Notes

Luke's account of the resurrection day offers the reader many details – who showed up first, what they saw, an explanation from an angel, how the disciples heard the news and how they reacted. Peter is still trying to piece together what Jesus said would happen with the confusing yet hopeful evidence of the empty tomb.

Clip Notes

Roomy Tomb (Clip 11): The scene opens with two tired, confused, frightened disciples who are trying to imagine what will happen next and what they should do. Confronted with the women's account of the empty tomb, they disbelieve it till they see for themselves. They're still confused, but hopeful too.

While all four gospels cover this most important event, each account is unique in some of the details. Ted and Lee stick most closely with Luke's story, but borrow from the others here and there. If you've watched the clips in succession, you'll hear some of their earlier lines repeated, this time with more hope. They've been asking lots of questions; now they're about to get some answers.

lesson outline

Describe a time when someone gave you news that was too good to believe, and how you reacted to it: Perhaps you got miffed at the messenger for teasing you ... or worked double-hard to not believe so you wouldn't be disappointed ... or refused to believe till you saw it for yourself.

Segue:

> After Jesus' execution, the disciples are in serious need of some good news. When some arrives, they don't know how to take it.

Show Clip 11, Roomy Tomb, then invite students to react to what they've just seen:

> Based on their behavior at the beginning of this scene, how do you think Pete and Andy are feeling?
>
> They seem to be expecting something awful to happen: What is it?
>
> Why don't they believe the women's story?
>
> Even after seeing the empty tomb, they can't quite figure out what's happened. Why don't they get it yet?
>
> Why do you suppose Pete says he's going fishing? What good will fishing do?

Read Luke 24:1-12, then discuss the passage:

> What have Ted and Lee added to the story that's not found in this passage?
>
> What does the passage tell us that the actors' have left out?

According to Luke, why do the disciples disbelieve the women's story about what they saw at the tomb?

If you were there when the women told the story, would you have reacted differently? What would you be thinking?

Would your view have changed if you had gone with Peter to see the empty tomb for yourself?

The passage ends with Peter still wondering what it all means. Why, after all he's heard and seen, is he still not getting it?

the next step

Pretend for a moment that this story went the other way: The women go to the tomb and find it just as they expected: undisturbed. They mourn his death for a week in Jerusalem, everyone packs up and returns home to Galilee, and once a year they return to the big city for Passover and place flowers in front of the tomb:

What does this do to the Bible?
What's your picture of Jesus? What's his purpose in your life?
What does this mean to your faith? To your hope of heaven?

(Tip: The Apostle Paul plays this very what if game in 1 Corinthians 15:13-20. If you have time, read his answers together.)

The fact is, the tomb *is* empty. Jesus is resurrected, and the news that's too good to believe is the very good news upon which our beliefs are built. But think about this: What if Jesus has *more* good news waiting for you to discover right now? You believe in the resurrection he promises, but what's a promise of his that you *don't* believe?

(Tip: Give an example here – something Jesus promises, but you have a hard time believing. Perhaps answer to specific prayer ... courage in a particular situation ...; then ask students to share their own answers).

What's preventing you from believing and acting on this promise?
What would change in your life if you did?

On the first day of the week, very early in the morning, the women took the spices they had prepared and went to the tomb. They found the stone rolled away from the tomb, but when they entered, they did not find the body of the Lord Jesus. While they were wondering about this, suddenly two men in clothes that gleamed like lightning stood beside them. In their fright the women bowed down with their faces to the ground, but the men said to them, "Why do you look for the living among the dead? He is not here; he has risen! Remember how he told you, while he was still with you in Galilee: 'The Son of Man must be delivered into the hands of sinful men, be crucified and on the third day be raised again.'" Then they remembered his words. When they came back from the tomb, they told all these things to the Eleven and to all the others. It was Mary Magdalene, Joanna, Mary the mother of James, and the others with them who told this to the apostles. But they did not believe the women, because their words seemed to them like nonsense. Peter, however, got up and ran to the tomb. Bending over, he saw the strips of linen lying by themselves, and he went away, wondering to himself what had happened.

—Luke 24:1-12 (NIV)

Beach Brunch

Lesson Twelve

passage: John 21:1-14

Teacher to Teacher

Review the exercise you did for the first lesson. (If you didn't do that lesson, do it now – it and this one are bookends.) Then take this lesson.

Reflect on these questions: How have the disciples changed as a result of their time with Jesus? How have they remained the same?

How have you changed most significantly since your first encounter with Jesus? What things haven't changed? What do you suppose will be the next big change in your life as a result of a growing faith?

Source Notes

John's gospel records one more encounter between Jesus and the fishermen on the Sea of Galilee. Like the first encountered (covered in Lesson 1), the disciples have had a long night with little success, which turns around dramatically after taking the advice of a stranger.

Clip Notes

Beach Brunch (Clip 12): Pete and Andy are fishing together again. Some things have changed, others are remarkably the same. Again they take the advice of a stranger and pull in a huge catch. But this time they recognize the Master Fisherman.

lesson outline

prologue

Describe something that soothes you — an activity that calms and refreshes you from the stresses of the world.

Segue:

> After an intense, difficult, amazing career as Jesus' disciples, Pete and Andy are back doing what they do best: fish.

the clip

Show Clip 12, Beach Brunch, then invite students to react to what they've just seen:

> How are Pete and Andy different in this scene than in previous clips?
>
> How are they the same?
>
> What would make them want to go fishing after all they've seen and done in their times with Jesus?
>
> How is it possible that after all that time they *still* don't recognize Jesus on the beach?
>
> How do they feel once they recognize him? What do you suppose they're thinking as they pull to shore?

the source

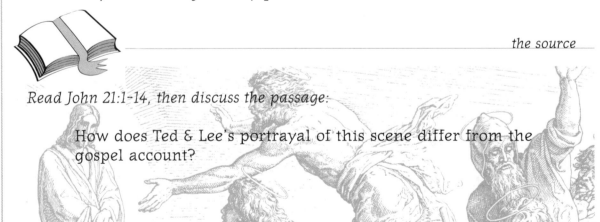

Read John 21:1-14, then discuss the passage:

> How does Ted & Lee's portrayal of this scene differ from the gospel account?

Does reading the passage change your view of the disciples? If so, how?

How do you suppose Jesus felt about catching his disciples back at their old job? Was he pleased? Disappointed?

Do they think differently about Jesus as a result of this episode? If so, how?

the next step

Where do *you* go to get away from life's pressures? What activity do you find most soothing in times of stress?

Can you think of a time when you stepped back from your faith, only to be surprised when Jesus showed up anyway? (Tip: Go first here with your own example.)

What does Jesus want you to know about him through this episode? How does that change your picture of him?

Afterward Jesus appeared again to his disciples, by the Sea of Tiberias. It happened this way: Simon Peter, Thomas (called Didymus), Nathanael from Cana in Galilee, the sons of Zebedee, and two other disciples were together. "I'm going out to fish," Simon Peter told them, and they said, "We'll go with you." So they went out and got into the boat, but that night they caught nothing. Early in the morning, Jesus stood on the shore, but the disciples did not realize that it was Jesus. He called out to them, "Friends, haven't you any fish?" "No," they answered. He said, "Throw your net on the right side of the boat and you will find some." When they did, they were unable to haul the net in because of the large number of fish. Then the disciple whom Jesus loved said to Peter, "It is the Lord!" As soon as Simon Peter heard him say, "It is the Lord," he wrapped his outer garment around him (for he had taken it off) and jumped into the water. The other disciples followed in the boat, towing the net full of fish, for they were not far from shore, about a hundred yards. When they landed, they saw a fire of burning coals there with fish on it, and some bread. Jesus said to them, "Bring some of the fish you have just caught." Simon Peter climbed aboard and dragged the net ashore. It was full of large fish, 153, but even with so many the net was not torn. Jesus said to them, "Come and have breakfast." None of the disciples dared ask him, "Who are you?" They knew it was the Lord. Jesus came, took the bread and gave it to them, and did the same with the fish. This was now the third time Jesus appeared to his disciples after he was raised from the dead.

—John 21:1-14 (NIV)

Resources from Youth Specialties

www.youthspecialties.com

Ideas Library
Ideas Library on CD-ROM 2.0
Administration, Publicity, & Fundraising
Camps, Retreats, Missions, & Service Ideas
Creative Meetings, Bible Lessons, & Worship Ideas
Crowd Breakers & Mixers
Discussion & Lesson Starters
Discussion & Lesson Starters 2
Drama, Skits, & Sketches
Drama, Skits, & Sketches 2
Drama, Skits, & Sketches 3
Games
Games 2
Games 3
Holiday Ideas
Special Events

Bible Curricula
Backstage Pass to the Bible Kit
Creative Bible Lessons from the Old Testament
Creative Bible Lessons in 1 & 2 Corinthians
Creative Bible Lessons in Galatians and Philippians
Creative Bible Lessons in John
Creative Bible Lessons in Romans
Creative Bible Lessons on the Life of Christ
Creative Bible Lessons on the Prophets
Creative Bible Lessons in Psalms
Wild Truth Bible Lessons
Wild Truth Bible Lessons 2
Wild Truth Bible Lessons—Pictures of God
Wild Truth Bible Lessons—Pictures of God 2
Wild Truth Bible Lessons—Dares from Jesus

Topical Curricula
Creative Junior High Programs from A to Z, Vol. 1 (A-M)
Creative Junior High Programs from A to Z, Vol. 2 (N-Z)
Girls: 10 Gutsy, God-Centered Sessions on Issues That Matter to Girls
Guys: 10 Fearless, Faith-Focused Sessions on Issues That Matter to Guys
Good Sex
The Justice Mission
Live the Life! Student Evangelism Training Kit
The Next Level Youth Leader's Kit

Roaring Lambs
So What Am I Gonna Do with My Life?
Game Resources
Games (Ideas Library)
Games 2 (Ideas Library)
Games 3 (Ideas Library)
Junior High Game Nights
More Junior High Game Nights
Play It!
Screen Play CD-ROM

Additional Programming Resources
(also see Discussion Starters)
The Book of Uncommon Prayers
Camps, Retreats, Missions, & Service Ideas (Ideas Library)
Creative Meetings, Bible Lessons, & Worship Ideas (Ideas Library)
Crowd Breakers & Mixers (Ideas Library)
Everyday Object Lessons
Great Fundraising Ideas for Youth Groups
More Great Fundraising Ideas for Youth Groups
Great Retreats for Youth Groups
Great Talk Outlines for Youth Ministry
Holiday Ideas (Ideas Library)
Incredible Questionnaires for Youth Ministry
Kickstarters
Memory Makers
Special Events (Ideas Library)
Videos That Teach
Videos That Teach 2
Worship Services for Youth Groups

Quick Question Books
Have You Ever...?
Name Your Favorite
Unfinished Sentences
What If...?
Would You Rather...?

Digital Resources
Clip Art Library Version 2.0 (CD-ROM)
Great Talk Outlines for Youth Ministry
Hot Illustrations CD-ROM
Ideas Library on CD-ROM 2.0
Screen Play

Youth Ministry Management Tools

Clip Art
Youth Group Activities (print)
Clip Art Library Version 2.0 (CD-ROM)

Professional Resources
Administration, Publicity, & Fundraising (Ideas Library)
Dynamic Communicators Workshop
Great Talk Outlines for Youth Ministry
Help! I'm a Junior High Youth Worker!
Help! I'm a Small Church Youth Worker!
Help! I'm a Small-Group Leader!
Help! I'm a Sunday School Teacher!
Help! I'm an Urban Youth Worker!
Help! I'm a Volunteer Youth Worker!
Hot Illustrations for Youth Talks
More Hot Illustrations for Youth Talks
Still More Hot Illustrations for Youth Talks
Hot Illustrations for Youth Talks 4
How to Expand Your Youth Ministry
How to Speak to Youth...and Keep Them Awake at the Same Time
Junior High Ministry (Updated & Expanded)
Just Shoot Me
Make 'Em Laugh!
The Ministry of Nurture
Postmodern Youth Ministry
Purpose-Driven® Youth Ministry
Purpose-Driven® Youth Ministry Training Kit
So That's Why I Keep Doing This!
Teaching the Bible Creatively
Your First Two Years in Youth Ministry
A Youth Ministry Crash Course
Youth Ministry Management Tools
The Youth Worker's Handbook to Family Ministry

Academic Resources
Four Views of Youth Ministry & the Church
Starting Right
Youth Ministry That Transforms